STILL Standing

STILL
Standing

MAKING *Progress* THROUGH THE *Process*

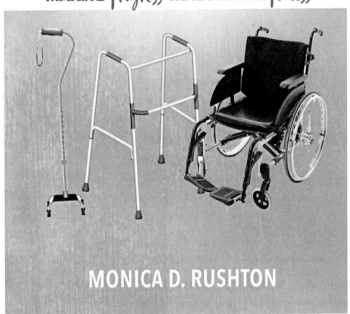

MONICA D. RUSHTON

INSCRIBED *Inspiration*

Published in Georgia by InSCRIBEd Inspiration, LLC.

All scripture references are taken from the public domain King James Version of the Holy Bible. The author suggests that readers review scriptures from other versions to supplement Biblical interpretation.

ISBN 13: 978-1-7338966-4-1

Cover Design: Soleil Branding Essentials

This book is a reflection of the author's life and experience. All stories are true and recorded to the best of the author's recollection. The author uses names with permission of those involved unless they have requested otherwise. There is mention of individuals who are deceased; family members have given permission for the use of their name. Details of some instances have been slightly modified to enhance readability, or to ensure privacy. Any resemblance of any other party is purely coincidental.

In Memory of

Denise F. Walker

Gone But Not Forgotten

Before I reached my 40th birthday I lost one of my closest friends — my mother! Her death was unexpected; God knew how much I could, and can still, bear. I was literally able to draw strength from the Word of God by meditating on the scripture, "To be absent from the body is to be present with the Lord (II Corinthians 5:8)." The Word of God continues to help me make it through my life without her!

The death of your mom is news you never want to hear, even though you know it is an inevitable part of life. My mother and I talked every day; several times a day. My sister Monique and Mom had a joke when the phone rang at their house, Monique would say, "It's Monica." When Aunt Arlene got the news she came to my house to tell me in person. I was shocked because I had just talked on the phone with my mother a little earlier that day.

My mom had challenges as a single mother but she persevered and no doubt did her best! As she got older her health began to present some challenges for her. To be quite honest, she shared some of her struggles with us and some she did not.

My mother was one of my biggest cheerleaders. She was always encouraging me to keep my faith, "Keep pressing your claim Monica." She told me, "MS for you means you are miraculously strong and mighty stylish." I will always remember her encouraging words.

Even though we only have memories of my mom to cherish, I am thankful to God that she doesn't have to be bogged down with adversities and trials of this life any longer!

Mother - July 16

It was the dimpled smile on your face, the style of your hair, your fashion and your own flair.
It was the touch of your hand, always willing to do whatcha could, you're listening ear always willing to hear!
It was your voice, your patience, and your faith that helps me know for sure you were in God's race.
Even helps me to understand, although you're no longer here you're in a much better place.
You know the place that we all dream about?
Hoping to get there, knowing there's no right time or place.
Ma, it's hard to accept but it was just your race to finish, ever too early or too late.
Just be ready when HE comes...

Daughter - July 11

STILL
Standing

Foreword

As a neurologist, when I think of Multiple Sclerosis (MS), I think of a disease that strips the insulation, called myelin, away from the nerves, and which causes various symptoms depending on what part of the central nervous system is involved. Because we have a good understanding of how the body's immune system causes this loss of myelin, we now have many medications that can slow, or even prevent, the loss of myelin. With this knowledge, I can educate people with MS, their families, and the general public about the disorder and the ways we have to treat it.

One thing I can't do, however, is to tell people what it's like to live with Multiple Sclerosis. I can see the changes Multiple Sclerosis causes in peoples' lives, and I can empathize with them. I can compare patients' experiences when they ask me. I can't describe the experience of having Multiple Sclerosis, however. Only someone who has lived with MS can do that.

I have known Mrs. Rushton for nearly 20 years. I have been able to see the changes in her life, both positive and negative. She brings clarity to me, and now to all of you reading this book, about her life experience with MS. She describes that experience from both her own personal standpoint, and that of other close people in her life. Mrs. Rushton comes at the disease positively, but also realistically. She lets us know that she can overcome the adversity that Multiple Sclerosis can cause.

It's one thing to know how the immune system has an effect on the nervous system. It is quite another, to understand the effect of this illness on a life. If you don't know someone with Multiple Sclerosis, you will after you read this book.

~Robert F. Richardson, Jr, M.D., FAAN
Assistant Clinical Professor of Medicine and Neurology,
Case Western Reserve University

Preface: MS Diagnosis

I graduated from the Mandel School of Applied Social Sciences in May of 1998; after two short years at the prestigious Case Western Reserve University! For the Masters Level degree in Social Science Administration I chose Health as my concentration. After six years of academic preparation, coupled with hands on field placements, I believed that I was ready to make a difference in the lives of others as a social worker.

Before participating in my commencement activities, I eagerly prepared for my job search by participating in a few mock interviews offered by the Career Center. Quite honestly, I wondered about finding a suitable job, but my faith kicked in and I trusted God to make a way for me to find employment. Thankfully the Executive Director of the agency where I worked as an intern from January through May offered me a salaried position! Thank God, my internship had become a full time position.

One or two months after starting my job I noticed something unusual while I was traveling to visit my grandmother. I was sitting at a traffic stop not far from her apartment complex when I recognized a slight difference in the brightness between my eyes. In one eye the red light appeared to look normal, but through my other eye the traffic light appeared dim. Recognizing that this was out of the ordinary, I made an appointment to see an ophthalmologist right away.

The doctor concluded that I had Optic Neuritis, a condition known as inflammation of the optic nerve. He shared with me, "Optic Neuritis could be an early sign of Multiple Sclerosis (MS)." The doctor calmly suggested, "Follow up with me in about six months or so."

I had never heard of Optic Neuritis, but I was familiar with MS; my cousin had been diagnosed as a teenager. I wasn't really worried about what the doctor had suggested about MS at that time because the diagnosis was a mere possibility for me. As a woman with strong faith I made a declaration: "I truly believe that no matter what, God is in control of my life; and man does not have the final say."

I was scheduled for a visual field test and one that required injecting dye to make sure there were no leaks inside of my eyes. Although these were just preliminary test measures, None of these tests provided conclusive evidence validating Multiple Sclerosis as a diagnosis for me.

After the medical appointments, I returned to my new job grateful that so far everything appeared to be fine. I was ready to complete the employee paperwork required by all new hires. I was able to maintain my everyday tasks as a Social Worker at the historical Friendly Inn Settlement.

Ironically, a few months after starting my job, I noticed visual changes that unnerved me while I was reading at a conference. After returning home I scheduled an appointment to have my eyes examined again. I hoped that the next examination would lead to more concrete information concerning Optic Neuritis.

The basic eye examination indicated noticeable vision changes from my previous examination. The ophthalmologist asked me, "Do you have any other medical problems or concerns?"

I reflected back to a time when I experienced tingling in my legs. I had dismissed it because the sensation did not last long. To my dismay, the ophthalmologist informed me, "Optic Neuritis and tingling in the legs are classic symptoms of Multiple Sclerosis." He scheduled me for a Magnetic Resource Imagining (MRI) scan, "It will be tedious and uncomfortable." I knew in my heart that this eye appointment was divinely orchestrated by God.

With the new information from the ophthalmologist, I could have started to think the worst about my situation. Secretly I was hopeful that MS was not the answer. I was only 26 years old at the time — my whole life was ahead of me.

In the year 2001 I was given concrete information that would change my life forever! My doctor reviewed the MRI results with me and I received the official diagnosis of Multiple Sclerosis. I remember saying to God, "Whatever my future holds, with YOU I know, I will make it!" The neurologist recommended that I start standard MS therapy quickly. All three of the medications were injectable: Avonex, Betaseron and Copaxone. The thought of self-injection was unthinkable for me, my tolerance for pain has always been low. I cringed at this recommendation!

Against my doctor's recommendation, and because of my fear of needles, I opted not to begin therapy right away. I was not feeling any effects of MS at the time; I did not think the medication was necessary. What I didn't know then, but understand better now, Multiple Sclerosis is called a "silent disease" for a serious reason. It progresses when a person does not see outward evidence. Medication is said to be effective at slowing down the progression of MS.

To date there is no known cure for Multiple Sclerosis, but I know that God has been with me in my journey. I wrote this book because I have a heartfelt desire to share my testimony. After all, this is how we overcome! We have to tell it! I believe that God's Word is true and Revelation 12:11 says, "And they overcame him by the blood of the Lamb, and by the word of their testimony…" My journey has not been easy; I have more lessons to learn about strengthening my confidence.

This is my story of learning to understand God's providence and accepting His will for my life.

Thank you for reading,

Monica D. Rushton

Rejoicing in hope; patient in tribulation;
continuing instant in prayer . . .
Romans 12:12 (KJV)

"This is my story of learning to understand God's providence and accepting His will for my life."

—Monica D. Rushton

Part I - Life With MS

"I Have Her Back"
(Sister Monique's Perspective)

I appreciate my sister Monica. Monica has positively impacted my life. I have no clue where I would be in my life right now if she were not my role model and confidante.

None of her deeds for me go unnoticed. I am truly blessed to have a sister like her. I love her for the 100,000,000 lil sacrifices she makes daily, for me and for others. My sister lends a listening ear and gives some of the best advice. It feels good to know she has my back. Monica is my big sister, my best friend and my angel in disguise. She is one of the strongest women I know. She is wise, beautiful and intelligent; I know God will bless her abundantly. I am thankful for Monica being herself. I admire her connection to God and her strong will. I love Monica and I am praying for her! We are going to kick some MS booty.

Leaning Into Support

Attending church is a big part of my family culture. After church our immediate family usually gathered at my Grandma's house for dinner. Someone would purchase a bucket of chicken to complement whatever Grandma had already prepared for us to eat. I personally tried to limit fried chicken from my diet on a regular basis, but honestly there were a few times when I gave in!

> "I had to learn to lean on my cane and much more for support."

Most Sundays my mom, sister, or auntie attended church with me. There were rare occasions when I felt confident and strong enough to attend church by myself. Around the year 2006 I had an incident after church. I was feeling physically weak and needed help to maneuver the steps from the church into the church parking lot. Thankfully there were family members there who walked me to my car.

That Monday morning I contacted my neurologist and scheduled a same-day appointment. It was a blessing that I was not working at the time. After the examination, the doctor recommended that I get a quad cane for daily usage, "It will help you maintain your balance." I purchased my cane from Lorraine Surgical Medical, that was quicker than ordering one and having it shipped to me.

Deep down inside I recognized that maintaining my independence was important to me. I admit that I did not want to walk with a cane, but as the saying goes, "A girl's got to do what a girl's got to do!" People would often ask me questions about why I used a cane. I really did not mind the questions. What I absolutely hated was when cars stopped or slowed down for me to walk across the street, or to the other side of a parking lot. I know it sounds a bit ridiculous, but that is honestly how I felt. I had to learn to lean on my cane and much more for support.

My Circle of Trust

When I was diagnosed with MS I did not want to tell anyone other than my immediate family; I knew they would pray for me. I conducted research to understand what the MS diagnosis meant for me. I kept a journal to record my thoughts, feelings, and prayers, but unfortunately, I no longer have it. That journal would have been a good way for me to compare where I am today with where I stood in my faith during those beginning stages of my diagnosis.

***

I found out that my high school friend Senequa and I share the same diagnosis! Senequa Poteat and I attended Warrensville Heights High School together. People used to say that we favored each other. I think it's because we both have big eyes, but that's my take. She graduated in 1991 and I graduated in 1992. Neither of our graduating classes were extraordinarily large in number, so pretty much everybody knew everybody!

Years after graduation, at the Warrensville Senior Civic Center, Senequa and I ran into each other at a Kym Sellers educational seminar. Kym Sellers is a media personality in the Cleveland, OH area who also has MS.

I can never have enough prayer partners — this woman of God is one of them! It is invaluable to me to have Senequa who is standing on the Word of God for

healing because she understands me. Senequa gets what I
am going through. Together we are
able to believe that He is more than
able to do exceedingly and
abundantly above all that we can
think or even imagine.

"God is Able"
(Best Friend Gina's Perspective)

Monica and I have a friendship and family connection that I would say was destined before we were born. I will share the background in a bit, but let me start by saying that Monica's love, faith, and inner spirit to celebrate life is rooted and sustained in the power of JESUS CHRIST. She shares His gentle nature and is a gifted encourager to many, despite her life's challenges and physical ailments. I am deeply inspired by her resilience – but not surprised, as the Monica that I know, continues to grow personally and professionally, while doing amazing things with, and for others. Our sisterhood is better for it.

Monica and I grew up together at Mt. Olive Missionary Baptist Church in Cleveland, OH. Our church was more than a religious institution. Our grand-parents attended Mt. Olive and our mothers: Denise Walker and Carol (Peters) Hughes grew up and prayed together. Their gifts of unconditional love and "family togetherness" was instilled in us. Monica and I are extremely close.

Mt. Olive became a life stream of people who genuinely cared about who we were, and who we would become. That support prepared us for handling life's circumstances. We were groomed and mentored by the Hattie Jackson Guild and Pam and Sam Shaw who were Young David's youth leaders. As young adults we were educated and "loved on" by Rev. Larry L. Harris, our youth pastor, and many other advocates who poured into our lives.

Who can forget – Grandma Laney's homemade rolls, the shared laughs and hugs, cards and good cheer exchanged at holiday times and birthdays? These generational blessings "breathe life" into us – even on our toughest days.

Monica has always been a get up and go, kind of sista-friend. She is never afraid to speak her mind or from her soul. Before her MS diagnosis, Monica and I were in one another's "Sister Circle." We were fashionistas who took shopping excursions, and were blessed to take trips across Ohio to gospel concerts and college campuses. We also enjoyed eating together at our favorite local spots.

Our life's journey took us over 1,200 miles apart when I moved to Texas for a season of my life. Monica and I continued to stay close. I learned recently that MS was impacting her day-to-day life. Monica was having "the shakes" while eating, experiencing frequent bathroom trips, and she was "feeling tired" at times. This information made me more sensitive to what she was experiencing.

Our youth pastor at Mt. Olive had MS, but I feel that (we as a culture) need more information about this disease and forms of treatment. This will help us be more supportive to those who have the disease. In elementary school I participated in a "jump-a-thon" to raise funds for MS research, but that was the extent of my knowledge. I am currently gathering information on my own using Internet resources, but I desire more filtered knowledge and expertise to support my friend.

Once Monica was diagnosed with MS, I can honestly express that our commitment to friendship and sisterhood was strengthened. While we are not able to see one another as often due her limited mobility, and my busy schedule, I treasure our meet-ups even more like the fantastic time in 2019 in Chicago (Chi-Town) with family and friends.

***

The Pink Fight

Did I tell you that Monica and I have a lot in common? With a life-threatening disease, I know how important it is to have someone praying for you and speaking positive words around you.

I transitioned to Atlanta, GA, the city of dreams, to be closer to family, friends and business opportunities. In January 2015, after moving, I was faced with a mountain that took a lot of prayer and support to survive. After what I thought was a routine mammogram, I was required to have additional screenings which confirmed that I had early stage breast cancer. I had no close family history of breast cancer and did not understand how I got it. Thank You JESUS CHRIST and "Obama Care." My team of doctors caught the disease early and were able to aggressively treat it with surgery and radiation therapy.

In addition to significant diet changes, more exercise, relaxation and more sleep on my part, I was healed. Over these last five years, I am thankful to be "cancer-free" and able to bring value to the lives of my family, friends and work clients. Monica is one of my closest supporters. She helped me move from surviving to thriving in my fight against breast cancer. I can declare with confidence, "It is not over until God says it is over." I believe in the power of scripture in Philippians 3: 13-14. I encourage you to read it in the King James and other versions because it is encouraging.

I will always remember and cherish the Christmas when Monica and her husband Tony donated to breast cancer research on my behalf. I displayed the card on our Christmas tree. Their monumental and awesome gift blew me away and transcended dollars. Their gift said to me, "I acknowledge your pain, I care enough to fight with you and encourage you not to give up."

It has been Monica's pure friendship and light in my life that has me loving life in the present. I consistently look forward to our next connection, text messages and shared family photos. These interactions aid me in staying on my journey of helping others. Our friendship encouraged me even through my divorce.

***

We are "sisters" of unlimited possibilities not disabilities and I love Monica. As we live our best life and discover God-given superpowers to enrich others, we will keep it moving!! God bless my sister Monica. She will continue to be an example of fighting MS with wisdom, grace, and great attitude.

Telling Friends

On a Sunday at my home church sometime in 2001, my pastor preached on women with MS and Lupus. It opened my heart and I thought to myself, "Maybe I should talk to Pastor Harris about my MS diagnosis." At the time I felt more comfortable with sharing my situation with people other than my family.

After reaching out to my Pastor I was free to talk with others about my diagnosis. I told my best friend Gina and I reached out to my college roommate Ebony. The first thing Ebony asked me was, "What scripture are you standing on Monica?" I had a big question mark on my forehead; Ebony's inquiry led me to think about the Word I was standing on figuratively and literally.

I had been listening to other people's testimonies of God healing them, yet I was not sharing my own testimony. Matthew 17:20 says, "And Jesus said unto them, because of your unbelief: for verily I say unto you, if ye have faith as a grain of **mustard seed** (author emphasis added), ye shall say unto this mountain, remove hence to yonder place; and it shall remove; and nothing shall be impossible unto you." This tells me that with a little faith, and no doubt, I can realize what seems impossible. This became a foundational scripture for my faith journey.

I told my testimony of the MS diagnosis to my friend Robin, another college classmate and she sent me a ministry tape from her church. Robin shared the scripture III John 2 with me, it says: "Beloved, I wish above all things that thou mayest prosper and be in health, even as thy soul prospereth." Robin gave me a scripture and Ebony asked a question; this was significant to my process and it changed my perspective.

I cannot walk this journey alone – I am grateful that these two women and other friends helped me to lean on my faith in God. They along with my family gave me courage to stand.

"She is a Pillar of Strength"
(Brother Marlon's Perspective)

I deeply love and appreciate my oldest sister Monica. She was the first of us to graduate from college and go to graduate school. I watched as Monica chose a career in social work and was thriving in her field while helping others.

I must admit that when she told me about her MS diagnosis, I was kind of in denial at first. It did not make sense to me how Monica was fully functioning but had MS. She was so young; I believed that nothing should be wrong with her, nor could I physically see any changes in her. In the beginning I did not understand the disease; I was the one always declaring, "You can overcome this Monica. You can fight it."

My lack of knowledge about MS and my denial that something was wrong with my sister prevented me from supporting her effectively in the beginning. What I could have done better was conduct research to understand the disease and its effects, and offer financial support if she needed it to investigate alternative medicines and therapy. If I would have known more at the time I would have done more and been more vocal. Even with Monica choosing not to take her medication for two years, I would have advocated against that decision.

For Monica to be so young and be dependent on others causes me to reflect deeply and emotionally. I know that if she could, Monica would get up and walk, she would dance, or get in the car and go see about other people. That is just the type of woman she has always been. I want my sister to have a phenomenal quality of life and I want her to recognize her contributions to the world. It inspires me that Monica continues to find ways to give back despite what she is experiencing personally.

One example of me observing Monica's strength is how she reacted to the catastrophic loss of our mother's passing. For Monica to be dealing with MS and be so strong despite her grief was inspiring to me; she and our mother were extremely close. I had to reflect on how I might have responded in that situation. If I had a disability I would probably have leveraged my mother's death to spiral downward, but I did not see that from my sister

Monica at all. I see her as an extremely strong woman and a pillar of strength through it all. Maybe Monica has moments where she probably wishes that things were different, but I have never seen that in her.

It is my honor as her brother to see Monica thrive – she is living with MS and she is truly not letting it impact her spirit.

Surrounded by Family Love

I cannot help but to reflect on how family has always been an important part of my MS journey. My siblings, aunts, uncles, friends and community members have been extremely supportive of me. As I mentioned earlier, one of my cousins was diagnosed with MS at the age of 16. I often wonder if there is a genetic link for the disease in my family.

At the beginning of my MS journey, some family members suggested that I take herbal supplements to help me manage my disease. One of those people was my cousin Marsha's husband. When Bernard learned of my diagnosis he and Marsha came to my home to give me Evening Primrose supplements. Bernard shared his experience with MS and how the supplements had improved his health. To God be the glory, Cousin Bernard is doing well today. Although I was grateful for them bringing the supplements to me, I didn't see a visible change so I stopped taking them after a few weeks.

There have been many other people who have stood with me along the way. Some have gone on to be with the Lord, but their love and Godly character lives on in my memories. One memorable person was Carol Henderson, a sweet woman of God whom I met while working at Highland Hills. Unfortunately she has since passed away, but I could never forget the impact she made in my life.

Carol initiated an individual consultation for me with her neuropathic doctor. I was not familiar with this practice, but I trusted Mrs. Henderson. I was blown away by her generosity and her willingness to invest in my health by paying for the recommended supplements after my initial visit.

After Ms. Carol showed support in this way, I put forth the effort to purchase additional supplements when I ran low. There were quite a few supplements required, and I was able to maintain some, not all of them.

My Aunt Tanya purchased flaxseed oil to supplement my diet. Literature speaks to flaxseed oil as being good for MS among other physical conditions. I started using it and I saw some significant results with my joints being more flexible! Flaxseed oil is another item I used for a time, then I put it on the back burner of must-haves. My aunts have all been examples of strength for me. Aunt Carol used to walk with me for exercise and Aunt Arlene has always pushed me to walk in faith.

My Uncle Dorian is another person who helped me during my MS journey. Uncle Dorian was the youngest of my mother's two brothers. He was friendly, kind-hearted, generous and loved to make people laugh. As Uncle Dorian's relationship with the Lord grew, he and I became close. His million-dollar smile still radiates in my heart.

I invited Uncle Dorian to be at my house when I began taking the injectable medication called Copaxone. It was necessary to have a nurse conduct a home visit to explain the process of taking the injection. I was happy

Uncle Dorian could be a part of the process; he kept the atmosphere light, kept me calm and helped me understand what the nurse was saying. It was a lot of information to absorb, but I was not worried or nervous with my uncle there with me.

Although I started with daily injections, I reasoned that because Copaxone required a much smaller needle I could handle doing it myself. It was a subcutaneous injection and came with a smaller needle than the other two! When the nurse was teaching me how to take the injection she explained, "The injection sites have to be rotated between the back of your arms, your thighs, upper buttocks and your stomach." We reviewed the pamphlets about the medication which advised of side effects.

To get through my daily injections, I had to encourage myself. I would say things like, "Monica, you can't allow fear to immobilize you or keep you from doing what the doctors are recommending." I would always affirm my faith in God and say out loud, "Monica, you are trusting God but He works through doctors and medications."

Initially I wrestled with the fact that the medication had to be mixed with a sterile vial of water. I was able to complete the intricate process of mixing it and injecting it into a syringe. I must say that it was a blessing for Copaxone users when prefilled syringes became available.

After being on Copaxone for a while I had an unpleasant experience with a side effect. I didn't realize that there was no timeline for side effects to manifest and that they could appear without warning. According to the advice of the nurse, heart palpitations were common. After one injection, round heart palpitations came upon me seemingly out of nowhere.

Experiencing heart palpitations was traumatic for me. I was nervous, but I knew enough to call on the name of Jesus. I first called 911 for help, and then I called my mother! When the ambulance arrived, I was sitting in the hallway of my apartment complex waiting for them. The emergency medical technician took my vitals and informed me, "Everything is normal." I had reacted to the heart palpitations, but I needed to allow time for the palpitations to subside.

I consulted my doctor about my experience right away. The heart palpitations along with the anxiety that I often experienced while being on the medication prompted me to stop taking Copaxone and try a different medication.

***

On October 4, 2019 another one of my supporters, my Uncle Howard passed away. Even though the occasion was hard to experience, it was a joy for me to spend time with my family at his homegoing service. A few weeks after Uncle Howard's homegoing, my mother's first cousin, Deborah, had a surprise seventieth birthday party. I was elated to attend the awesome kid-friendly celebration with my sister and my nieces.

There were many family members in attendance. I couldn't have a conversation with them all, but I could hug and kiss everyone from my wheelchair. To God be the Glory! I was able to dispel the myth that I am confined to my wheelchair. Some of my family members did not know that I can still get around with my walker.

Coincidentally, I sat at a table with Aunt Arlene and a few cousins. I was eager to join this table of family members because it gave me a chance to share my testimony with my cousin Angela. I grew up singing in the Sims Family Choir and I would hear Angela talk at concerts about Revelation 12:11, "we overcome by the blood of the lamb and the word of our testimony."

I was elated to say to Angela, "I didn't quite grasp in totality the meaning of Revelation 12:11 as a child. As an adult, I have a totally different understanding and reassurance as I stand on this specific word of God! Not only am I able to share my testimony, I am able to embrace and encourage the testimonies of others." In the photo below my Cousin Angela is wearing white. Next to her is Cousin Yvonne, Aunt Arlene and then me.

I told Angela, "Revelations 12:11 is giving me boldness to share my ups and downs with MS. I have held on to the memory of you sharing this scripture for

all of these years. When I lean on my faith, I remember that I am more than a conqueror." I shared with her how grateful I was for her faith.

Share Your Testimony with Confidence

If you have a hard diagnosis, I believe it is important to share the difficult situations with people you trust. You may be nervous, but you will feel much better at the end of the conversation. I want to share some things I learned from my circle of trust:

1. Talk about the difficult things you are experiencing with people you know will pray for you, and with you.
2. You don't have to take every suggestion your family and friends offer, but allow them to help you. They want to see you thrive.
3. Listen to the testimonies of the people around you. It will not only strengthen them, but it strengthens your faith too.
4. Stand on a scripture for every circumstance.

"She is Resilient"
(Aunt Arlene's Perspective)

It's one thing for a person to go through something as an individual; but their family goes through it with them. I think my sister told me about Monica's diagnosis. I knew something was going on, but there was not a name put to it yet. Monica was having issues with her eyes, tingling in her limbs and that kind of stuff, but from my perspective, nothing life threatening was discussed. Even when Monica lived with me for a while I did not see any MS symptoms. After she moved out on her own, these things began to be more prevalent.

Monica was still driving, shopping and operating normally in her daily life during that time. I would hear her make comments like, "There is a film over my eyes," or, "I'm not seeing too well." I was not focused on the fact that she was having health problems. Once we as a family learned that Monica had MS, it hit us like a blow. When it got a name we all expressed, "She seemed okay."

From my perspective, Monica's life has been a faith walk in every aspect. MS is a really significant part of that walk. Prior to her MS diagnosis, Monica was trying to stay true to her faith in Christ and she carried herself accordingly. The MS diagnosis and the phases of MS she is experiencing are tests of her faith.

After learning her diagnosis, Monica felt that because things were going well she could stop taking her medication. On top of feeling well, she was having side effects including anxiety and high blood pressure which caused her to stop her regimen without telling us.

I would have told her to take her medication. I would have probably said, "Monica that's not a good idea." Sure Monica didn't look sick, and she says that she consulted with her neurologist to make the decision. Monica told me that she only looked at what she could see at the time. I don't think her faith has ever wavered even though she did ask a lot of questions. I watched MS play out in Monica's life and it reminded me of my friend's sister. I thought, "If Monica sticks with her medication, she will be cool." I did not learn she stopped taking it until she was off of it for a year.

***

The sister of one of my dear friends has lived with MS for over fifty years. She is 78 now, but during the time of her diagnosis they did not have the medications that exist now. As a young woman I saw my friend's sister experience a lot of stages in her MS. She was swollen from steroids; had weight fluctuations; was blind for a while; regained her sight; and went from walking with a cane to a wheelchair. MS has debilitated my friend's sister.

I believe in the beginning Monica was in denial about her disease. I understood her faith and her trust in God so I did not press her. I thought she was taking her medication. I didn't want to tell Monica that God had not healed her; but there was a nagging in the back of my mind about her well-being. I know that some of what Monica is dealing with may have been alleviated if she had stayed on her medication. God is able, but He gives us the sense to do what we are supposed to do.

I stumbled.

After a period of taking my medications, I began to feel better. I proclaimed to myself, "Thank God I'm free!" I did not look sick, nor did I feel sick, so I surmised that I did not need my injections. Without telling anyone, I stopped taking them. I did not recognize that I was living with a disease that is incurable, yet manageable.

My Aunt Arlene calls the time of me being off of my medication "the stumble." I lost focus because I did not stick to the plan my physicians gave me. I lost focus of the management plan and let it go. Unfortunately, I was not managing my disease well.

When I finally got around to scheduling an appointment to discuss a medication change with my neurologist he told me, "This is how you know the medication is working, you don't have any issues which are commonly known as a relapse."

I asked my neurologist, "Why do I have to take this medication?" This was my attempt at consulting with him to stop my prescriptions all together. "I am fine."

He suggested, "Go on a medication that you have to take three times a week and not every day."

To that I mentally said, "No thank you." I went forward with my plan not to take medication. I did not take my medication for two years. Clearly, I wasn't thinking!

What did that decision mean to me at the time? It heightened the potential for me to digress with my healing.

I thought I was good, but MS was still in my body even after I stopped taking the medication. I was thinking everything was good and that I was healing, but MS was still with me.

When an opportunity came for me to try a new medication I did not hesitate. I have been on four different medications. At one time I tried an oral pill when I went to rehab because I did not want to take injections any longer. Unfortunately, I had to go back to an injectable medication, which I hated. I have stopped and started on so many medications that I am pretty sure it has effected the course of my disease progression.

Back on Track

One day while I was on my way to have an examination with the State Physician for my disability approval I fell unexpectedly in the elevator at Southpoint Hospital. I was not walking with my cane at that time and I literally could not get up after the fall. Some people that I did not know had to help me get up. That was a literal example of a stumble that required me to get back on track.

I remember that 2006 was a high-stress time for me. After being off of my medication for two years I started to feel sick again. I began to reflect on my decision to stop my regimen and one day at church I decided to have a church Elder pray for me. I told her "I have MS and I have been off of my medication for a while. Right now I am struggling with whether or not it is the right decision."

I'll never forget that before she prayed, she asked me, "Who told you to stop taking your medication?" A few days after that prayer I reconsidered my decision and decided to take my treatment more seriously.

Not long after that experience at church I was driving to work in downtown Cleveland. I pulled into the parking garage and when I got out of my car something felt unfamiliar; everything was spinning around me. I was experiencing vertigo. I had recently started a new job and my health insurance was not active. I had to deal with vertigo without seeing my doctor or getting medication.

I was terminated from my job just before my six month probationary period. My position was stressful and I honestly felt okay with their decision to let me go; I did not feel that I was a good fit for the company. The blessing in the termination was that I was offered COBRA insurance. This insurance permitted me to go to Cleveland Clinic for an appointment.

At the aforementioned appointment with Cleveland Clinic I saw an MRI scan for the first time. I was astonished that this particular MRI of my brain showed several lesions on my brain. When I was first diagnosed with MS the doctors told me I had a *few* spots of inflammation on my brain. One doctor said, "The initial onset is a pretty good prediction of the course that the disease might take."

God allowed the doctors to show me a healthy brain for comparison. I didn't take the hint at the time that there was a difference in the healthy brain and the brain of the one who had MS. I still did not share with a lot of people what was happening with me due to my own MS diagnosis.

I learned from another African American woman living with MS that a doctor cannot make a projection about how MS can effect someone. On one hand they say it's unpredictable, but on the other hand they offer their best educated guess!

***

How does an able bodied and faith filled woman like me choose denial? As my Aunt Arlene says, I chose to ignore ". . . what was being said and shown." She asked me, "What was the point of going to the doctor if you weren't going to listen to what he was saying?" True enough, medicine is a practice and everything isn't what it seems, but the MRI was tangible evidence.

I don't know if I made a conscious decision to deny my diagnosis because I had not seen my MRI results when I was initially diagnosed in 2001. Fast forward to the MRI in 2006, there was a big difference in five years. The doctor told me to consider a different medication, "If you were my family member I would want you to be on Avonex."

Reflecting back on every nuance and aspect of my journey is sometimes overwhelming. I know that God has, and is still keeping me. I hope that my stumbles will remind you to STICK TO YOUR PLAN. Yes, God is able, but you have to do what they tell you to do. This diligence will prevent you from experiencing some of the things I experienced because I veered off of my plan.

As I write this, I am taking a medication that has kept me off of steroid treatments for six years to God be the Glory! I am still standing!

Trust in the Lord with all thine heart; and lean not unto thine own understanding. In all thy ways acknowledge him, and he shall direct thy paths.
Proverbs 3:5-6 King James (KJV)

"I know that God has, and is still keeping me."

-Monica D. Rushton

Rededicated to my Health

Upon restarting my medication I had a renewed vision to manage my disease. Although I've always believed that exercise is important, I've never been a fan of gyms or lifting weights. I enjoy breathing fresh air. It was a great exercise to walk the trails at a local park.

As I mentioned, some mornings my Aunt Carol and I would get up early and walk together. We put forth the effort to establish a consistent routine, but eventually we had to stop. It seemed that after exerting a certain amount of physical energy I would experience a tingling sensation in my legs and that made me uncomfortable. I'm not sure if this is normal after exercising, but having nerve ending issues related to MS, it was not a good feeling for me. Actually, it was quite frustrating.

I began to explore other physical activities that could be more suitable for me. One such activity was joining my cousin Tiffany at an exercise program geared toward women. This was definitely an incentive for me, I didn't like to work out alone. I purchased a membership at a location in my neighborhood. I was motivated to go regularly; I didn't want to waste my money! I joined with the hopes that my cousin and I could work out together. Unfortunately our schedules never coincided, so we never worked out together.

The atmosphere was inviting in the gym and I felt comfortable enough to exercise without a partner. I enjoyed the helpfulness of the staff. I was extremely motivated because I saw results in a decrease in pounds and inches. My efforts were paying off and I felt good about my progress.

After going to the gym for a while, I found myself facing a similar dilemma with tingling in my limbs that felt overwhelming. I talked with my neurologist and explained my concerns. He wrote a letter to the program that released me from being financially penalized because I needed to withdraw.

Believe it or not, I tried water exercise too. The MS Society offered financial waivers for an MS class offered at a community center near my home. Knowing that I wasn't alone in this MS fight gave me hope. What a blessing it was to still be able to drive at the time; I was able to attend classes regularly!

I found it fascinating to be a part of a group facing the same, or similar physical challenges. The class reminded me of a water aerobics class I attended with my grandmother. Water exercise is good at any age; this intergenerational water aerobics class proved that fact!

Just when I thought I had finally found the perfect exercise regimen, I started to struggle with a different issue. I'm not sure of the technical jargon that would explain exactly what I experienced, but it had nothing to do with tingling. After completing my exercise routine and proceeding to get out of the water, there were no problems. My ability to walk to the locker room was a different story. My legs felt heavy as if someone was pulling me down! I was dealing with lack of balance and coordination. This is called Ataxia. Sometimes it is apparent and other times it is not. Needless to say I participated infrequently in these exercise classes after these types of episodes.

I had to find a new way to stay on track with managing my MS. In either case, I was standing on God's promises for my life.

Helpful Tips for Family and Friends

I have been living with MS for several years. It was not always easy for me to ask for help and support when I needed it. If you have a family member or a friend with MS, here are a few ways you may be able to offer support to your loved one:

1. Ask what your loved one can do on their own. Do not assume his or her limitations.
2. A phone call will help you understand firsthand how your loved one is doing. Don't hesitate to share good news about yourself or people you know mutually. This can be encouraging for them.
3. Educate yourself about the disease they are living with.
4. Ask if them if they have specific prayer requests and keep your loved one lifted in prayer.
5. When possible, support efforts to fight against any disease by volunteering your time or making a monetary donation to credible organizations.

These are my suggestions, but I am sure your loved one would appreciate your attempt to reach out to them in your own way. Consider making a list of things you would like to do and what your loved one requests of you.

Ways I Can Support _____

(Write name here)

_____

_____

_____

_____

_____

_____

_____

_____

_____

_____

_____

_____

_____

_____

_____

_____

_____

_____

_____

_____

Ways I Can Support _____

_____

_____

_____

_____

_____

_____

_____

_____

_____

_____

_____

_____

_____

_____

_____

_____

_____

Part II – Love Never Fails

Lunch with a Friend

On April 7, 2011 I had an appointment to get my 2005 Mitsubishi Galant detailed. My cousin Bianca obliged my request for a ride to pick up my car. To my surprise, when the detail specialist introduced himself he walked me to my vehicle.

I must admit, I was intrigued by his courteous and friendly disposition. We decided to exchange telephone numbers and spoke later that day. During the conversation we shared our spiritual beliefs and perspectives that centered on the Word of God. After an hour-long conversation, I felt a sense of commonality and perhaps the opportunity for a friendship to develop.

Surprisingly, I did something I've never done before — I asked him out. This was a kind gesture because I had not given him a tip for his detail services. I said to him, "On your next day off, I want to treat you to lunch." I wanted it to show appreciation and gratitude for a job well done. I was not asking him out on a "date."

I suggested a light meal such as soup, or a turkey wrap at a quaint restaurant I liked. He enjoyed the meal and frozen yogurt was our tasty treat for dessert. After lunch we decided go shopping; I must admit shopping is one of my favorite things to do. Tony wanted to look for new tennis shoes and I felt I could be of assistance to him. I'm not sure I was much help, but he found a pair that he liked and I found a pair of sandals. We left the store as two happy shoppers! I said to him, "This was a nice day Tony, maybe we can do it again sometime."

After the initial outing, it wasn't hard to believe that we would connect for an official date. I was eager to accept Tony's dinner invitation when he asked. We went to a Mexican restaurant that I rarely dined in, and I enjoy Mexican food. Our seating arrangement was quite unique in my opinion, he chose to sit beside me as opposed to across from me. I found it odd, but cute and romantic at the same time!

Our dinner conversation was interesting. We were quickly approaching our first shared holiday as friends and discussion was around what our Easter plans would be! I shared with him, "I just moved into a new apartment and everyone is coming to my home." My plan was to attend church on Resurrection Sunday and have dinner afterward with my family.

We had already planned to attend Sunday morning service together at Pentecostal Church of Christ with Bishop Delano Ellis. I was familiar with the church, but had never attended a Sunday service. Honestly, I had been to a few services of this particular denomination and I felt comfortable there. After church Tony and I agreed that the service was gratifying to our spirits and perhaps we would visit again. I invited him to dinner; I decided it would be a great time to introduce my new friend to my family.

Everybody pitched in and prepared an Easter dish. It was easy to eat with a hassle-free cleanup! I prepared one of my favorites, macaroni and cheese. The first time I made it for a family holiday, Uncle Dorian bragged on how good it was. Actually in his humorous way, he called it the "lock up." Of course we all giggled. My family graciously welcomed Tony and introduced themselves. I'm not sure if Tony was nervous or not, but I distinctly remember him focusing his full attention on me.

Commitment and Marriage

In my heart, I knew one day I'd be up for the challenges of marriage. I honed in on the scripture from Proverbs 18:22: "Whoso findeth a wife findeth a good thing, and obtaineth favour of the Lord." My parents were never married, and my first marriage role models where my grandparents. After college and Graduate School, I believed I was spiritually and emotionally prepared to be a wife. I eagerly waited for the opportunity to say yes to a sincere proposal. In my eyes spiritual compatibility, emotional maturity and financial responsibility were all significant to marriage! In fact these were all absolutely essential.

Looking back, I can honestly say that I was happy for various friends who had said "Yes!" to the wedding dress and "I do" to their husbands! As I pondered over when I might have the same opportunity, I often asked my mom, "Why am I last?" Deep down inside I believed that neither of us are able to control God's timing.

***

As time progressed, Tony and I decided to begin a committed courtship. Our first priority was to find a church home. Premarital counseling was definitely on our radar and Friends Church in Willoughby Hills offered a free twelve-week session. We enrolled in the class and visited their Sunday services regularly.

I wasn't sure why, but one particular Sunday after service we drove to Richmond Mall. I followed Tony's lead. It was a good thing for me that the mall wasn't crowded. I was walking with a quad cane at the time and avoiding crowded areas as much as possible helped me maintain a level of comfort. To my surprise Tony led me into Kay Jewelers! We had previously discussed engagement rings that we liked but I must say I was definitely caught off guard that day. I did not know Tony had been planning this special time!

The sales representative was helpful and showed us a variety of engagement rings. Tony beamed, "Pick the one you like." I tried on several rings and I picked a princess-cut diamond, something I never thought I wanted, but my instincts said it was the one! I had a slight tingling sensation on my finger, or so I thought. *How can I go wrong with this choice,* I pondered?

In February 2012 my husband-to-be proposed to me. Tony and I courted for approximately 15 months and we talked about setting a wedding date for July or August 2012. I couldn't believe that my turn had finally come to get married! We wanted to make sure he had enough time to purchase the ring we selected together. I knew other married women with MS so I never feared that having this disease would prevent my chances of having marital bliss.

Commitment Ceremony

Initially I really wanted a destination wedding somewhere tropical, but I don't think it mattered to my fiancé. As a dutiful wife-to-be, I took the lead on planning and began a Google search. First on my radar was on a popular resort. I found that they offered many wedding packages. At first I thought St. Lucia would be a great location for our wedding ceremony but their payment deadlines did not work well with our budget.

I kept searching and decided a water-based theme would be comparable. This is how Las Vegas came to our attention. After reviewing the wedding packages and prices of a popular resort, we decided to book our airplane tickets. We openly shared our plans from the beginning that Las Vegas would be our intended destination for a private ceremony. Things were coming together and we were eagerly anticipating our wedding day, Friday, July 27, 2012. We were excited to book the Shark Reef Aquarium for the official day to commit and pledge our eternal love. Once we got there, I was totally convinced that this option was the most creative and romantic.

Although, the backdrop for the ceremony was not what I would call tropical without a beach nearby, I felt that the first time experience of looking at the fish and sharks through the aquarium glass would be beautiful for us both! While I had never been to Las Vegas before, nor an Aquarium, Tony had never flown on an airplane. We were convinced that even though our family and friends wouldn't be able to share with us on our special day, we carried them in our hearts and knew that our day would be uniquely memorable for sure!

We were almost at the finish line and unfortunately I lost my driver's license on the airplane! On top of that major disappointment, I had left my cane in the car. We called the airport but my license was never recovered. Thankfully, without a marriage license we could have a commitment ceremony. Would I walk down the aisle alone or would my groom escort me?

I don't think either of us really realized the fact that I was walking without my cane. The ceremony was captured on video so there is evidence that we walked down the aisle together without my quad. Oh, to God be all the glory. I didn't consciously choose to leave it in the car, but that's where it stayed until we returned a day later.

We both believed the ceremony was beautiful! The minister and photographer added character and a bit of pizzazz as I like to say, to our day. After we took several photographs, we enjoyed a prepared lunch from room service. I had salmon which is one of my favorites, and Tony had his favorite meal, chicken alfredo.

While in Vegas we begin to make preparations for holy matrimony services in Cleveland. Our schedule was pretty tight but we had to start somewhere. My twentieth class reunion was taking place on August 4, 2012. On this same day my family hosted a cookout at the park. Obviously we could not be in two places at the same time so we had to prioritize!

On August 4 we had a small wedding at the home of Mr. and Mrs. Rushton, Tony's parents in Youngstown, OH. We were married by their pastor and he signed our marriage license. I was happy and grateful that my mom was able to travel with us to witness the ceremony!

Tony and I were excited to start our new life together. Little did we know, just six months later, in February of 2013, our lives would be presented with an unexpected shift!

And all things, whatsoever ye shall ask in prayer, believing,
ye shall receive.
Matthew 21:22 (KJV)

"I knew other married women with MS . . . I never feared that this disease would prevent my chances of having marital bliss."

–Monica D. Rushton

In Sickness and in Health

I worked part-time as an activities coordinator for the senior citizens at Highland Hills. I felt blessed with my new husband and my supervisor who understood my physical challenges with MS.

I pressed my way daily and enjoyed going to work. One of the things I enjoyed was monitoring a line dance class for the seniors in the ballroom. I was able to go up and down stairs to the ballroom. At that time I could actually do some of the line dances, but I chose not to. I thank God they had an elevator for the times when I felt overly tired.

My cousin David was a resident at Highland Hills. He donated my great-great aunt Pauline's motorized chair to the facility. At times that chair lightened the load for me while I was at work. I never had to worry about being able to do things like get to the restroom quickly or move around to different parts of the facility.

What a blessing.

MS Flare Up: February 2013

On February 2, 2013, I had an appointment with my neurologist. My mom was able to drive me, I felt too weak to drive myself. After what I thought was a normal examination, I was admitted for a two-day inpatient stay at the hospital until I could be transferred to a rehab facility of my choice.

As a licensed social worker I was familiar with the intake process and patient assessments, but I was on the other side of being a helper. There were many questions to answer, but having my husband with me made me feel at ease. Who would have thought a routine visit to the doctor would begin my rehabilitation journey? It is amazing how circumstances change within a blink of an eye.

I found comfort knowing that I was close to home at a community hospital, but staying overnight in a hospital is not comforting at all. Although I was familiar with hospitals, oddly enough I felt like I was in a strange place with no sense of direction or purpose. I was happy to receive visits from a few coworkers during their lunch breaks. Honestly their visits made me wonder when I would be able to return to my own work.

My doctor had arranged for my transfer to Metro Health Rehabilitation Center on the west side of Cleveland. I was disappointed. This would be a longer commute for my husband, family and friends to visit me. Because I had experienced outpatient physical therapy at their facility I believed I would be satisfied with Metro's care.

My hospital room reminded me of my college dorm – lots of closet space for personal items. I was not sure of how long I would have to stay, but Tony made sure I had everything I needed: toiletries, pajamas, comfortable shoes, loose fitting pants, joggings suits and tops.

Since I was a newlywed, I felt a sense of loneliness when visiting hours were over and my husband had left for the night. I knew my Heavenly Father was my source of strength and would see me through. I was able to meditate with music and some of my favorite songs. Thankfully I had a private room so was able to play gospel music all night long. I must admit, it was soothing to my soul.

In an effort to fortify my spirit and encourage my heart I saturated the airways with two of my favorite songs. I absolutely love the songs "Life and Favor" by John P. Kee and "Take Me to the King" by Tamela Mann. I played these two songs, especially at night when I slept. I meditated night and day on these lyrics.

Sleeping for rest is important, but resting in the assurance that my Heavenly father would see me through these new life challenges is where I really needed to rest my mind. I had a peaceful night's rest that first evening.

Scheduled Rehab and Physical Therapy Activities

I always woke up early, eager to be fully dressed before anyone entered my room. With therapeutic activities my day began at 8:30 with breakfast and therapy at 9. I usually started with physical therapy. I enjoyed occupational therapy because I worked on completing practical tasks. Speech therapy was not regularly on my schedule; art therapy was offered almost every day if I chose to participate. I always liked arts and crafts so I was happy to complete at least two art projects that I brought home with me.

I traced a butterfly and painted it purple with pretty green and orange as a contrast. I now have it on my refrigerator door as reminder that I was able to make something beautiful even though I was in a dark place. This is the butterfly I use to remind me of the declaration: STILL STANDING. I learned later that an MRI of the brain is shaped like a butterfly.

Rehabilitation at Night

Ataxia is the technical term for lack of balance and coordination. I was diagnosed with 4- limb ataxia, but initially it was not obvious. I have unsteady hands, I am not always able to feed myself, cook, or write legibly. For safety measures, I wore a bracelet indicating that I was a fall risk! During the day I didn't feel too restricted while actively participating in activities and walking with a walker to the restroom when necessary.

After therapy, returning to my room meant that I was ready to have dinner, receive visitors, return phone calls, or participate in an activity if I chose to do so. By this time one of the nighttime nurses was available to assist me with showering. By the evening time I was grateful that I had made it through another day. I was eagerly anticipating the next day if God allowed.

I've always had upper body strength; however my lower extremities were problematic. As long as I was in a seated position I could dress independently. These are normal everyday tasks for many people that can easily be taken for granted, but for me I felt empowered to be able to accomplish them! I definitely put forth a lot of effort to see things optimistically speaking, but at night it was hard. If I needed to use the bedside commode I had to notify the nurse and wait for a staff member to assist me.

I've wrestled with the nuances of frequent urination, increased urgency, and the inability to void at times. I called for assistance quite often. Sometimes assistance was quick to come, then and only then was I was able to relieve myself! Unfortunately, there were times when I had to wait. This to me, was the worst part of being considered a fall risk.

Continuity of care is important in a healthcare setting. Therefore, familiarity of both day and night staff is helpful along with a daily routine. I was becoming accustomed to the daytime routine, but I struggled at night. Going to sleep without my husband was challenging. I called him every night and sometimes in the middle of the night. I knew I was interrupting his sleep, but I couldn't help myself. He listened as long as he could. Yes, in some ways I just needed a pacifier!

Valentine's Day 2013

After I was admitted into rehab we soon realized that God is in control! Clearly our faith was being tested. Some say that God has a sense of humor but I agree with Romans 8:28: "And we know all things work together for the good of those who love the Lord and have been called according to His purpose." That scripture came alive for me when a group of seniors from Highland Hills Senior Community surprised little ole me with a visit.

As the Activities Coordinator for Highland Hills Senior Department, I often planned group visits for the community residents who were in the hospital. Words cannot describe the warmth and elation I felt in my heart to see their faces.

That visit was so encouraging that it gave me strength to focus on my primary rehab goals and objectives. It reminded me of the exercise and balancing classes that I led for them every Tuesday. The seniors would do better than me sometimes. Because of their consistency and commitment to our class it was a reminder to draw strength from their dedication.

One of my therapy goals was to work with a speech therapist. I don't recall a lot about this particular therapy, or how many times I actually participated during my inpatient stay. As I reflect, what stands out vividly is the difficulty I had trying to answer the therapist's question. She was adamant about me remembering what day it was and kept asking, "What is special about today's date?"

The verbal cues she gave didn't help. When I figured out it was Valentine's day, I realized why I was clueless. For most folks February 14th is Valentine's Day, but for me it was special because it was my Grandma's birthday! Unfortunately, Grandma passed away on February 1, 2010 just shy of her 80th birthday. My Grandmother was such a special lady and I cherish the love we shared to this day. With her being gone, I had a hard time differentiating between the two dates; they were synonymous to me for many years.

Considering that this was a Valentine's Day, it was not easy to be away from home but I did feel loved and appreciated. That Valentine's day I was pleasantly surprised with a visit by one of my coworkers who brought flowers and a card from the Highland Hills staff. This young lady was one of the clerical staff members, but we affectionately called her "Candy Girl" because her desk always had a full candy dish. I'm not exactly sure how long I had been away from work, but it was clear that I was not forgotten! I trusted that my coworker would extend my heartfelt gratitude to our colleagues for their kindness when she returned to work.

I expected my husband to make his way to the hospital as soon as he could. That year I celebrated Valentine's Day as a newlywed! This was my own personal jubilee and it was unique because of birthday memories with Grandma. I was bedazzled with flowers, chocolate, and a stuffed animal holding a flower! I loved all my gifts, but what I really wanted for Valentine's Day was to be home with my new husband.

Being in rehab was a necessary part of my healing process. Here are some things I want to share about getting through the experience:

1. Make a list of songs that help you worship God. When you feel down or discouraged, play your songs and allow God to soothe your soul.
2. Follow through with your therapy goals. It won't always be easy, but it will strengthen you.
3. Allow people to come visit you who bring you joy and can pray for you. Their presence will fortify you.

"Last Things First"
(Husband Tony's Perspective)

I take care of my wife. When she was in rehab it was no question that I would step up and be there for her. Monica always tells people, "It was comforting for me to know that he would just listen to me. I felt detached and disoriented. I wasn't able to have the comfort of my husband who loves me no matter what. I could not cook or feed myself and it was hard not being able to hug, kiss, or wake up to him."

During her February 2013 rehab stay I went to the hospital, curled her hair, did her pedicures and manicures, washed and ironed her clothes. Those are tangible things, but Monica says it warms her heart that I used to take her calls at night. She would call me at night when she knew I was home. I worked during the day and sometimes she would call me when I was asleep.

They let me stay at the hospital one time out of the four months she was there, but I was meticulous about making sure everything was right for her. I checked everything in that room. One day I found mold under the eating tray. I pointed it out to my wife and she didn't know she was eating like that. I told the staff, "I don't live like this at home and I didn't bring my wife here for her to live like this either."

I guess I was too aggressive. The doctor insinuated to my wife that I was harming her at home. He asked a lot of questions and came at her as if she was mentally unstable by allowing me to talk to her in the way I did.

I called a meeting with that doctor to correct the fact that he disrespected my wife and I wore a suit to the meeting. I told him, "My wife is an intelligent woman. She has a degree in Social Work and is licensed. Monica can handle her business and do it well." The doctor apologized to me; he knew he was out of character and had made an incorrect judgement about me, AND my wife.

***

One morning while Monica was in rehab I got locked out of our house. I had so much on my plate thinking about my wife and I left my keys in the house on accident. Because I don't like to be late I decided to walk the four miles to work and worry about my keys afterward. My job as head car detail specialist was close to home but I still made an effort to be an hour early every day. I liked to get myself settled, pray and meditate before I started working. I got up at 5:30 every morning.

After work I went to visit Monica to tell her what had happened and then I had to use my tools to get back into the house. I was tired after that long day. It was crazy because during that time I had misplaced my cell phone and could not call anyone. I did not get my phone back until two or three months later when a customer called to tell me that it was in his car.

***

Last Things First.

When Monica first got ill her mother came and stayed with us. She was there during the day to help around the house and take care of her while I was at work. One day Monica was so weak that she fell and my mother-in-law could not pick her up. She called me at work, "Monica fell and I can't get her up."

I told my boss what happened and he seemed reluctant to let me go home. "This is my wife; I will never get anything close to this again. I want to cherish this moment. I am going home." I honor my wife.

He asked me something crazy like, "Why did you marry a woman with health problems?"

"I don't know about the relationship you have with your wife, but I cherish what I have and I can't replace her. I don't know how you feel about yours, but I know how I feel about mine. I have to go." I gave him his keys and quit that day.

I got home an hour later. For a while they called me back to work but I didn't go. Eventually they wore me down with offers and a raise. To God be the glory! I know that I made the right decision that day. The man who asked me why I married the wife I did is now divorced. His business is gone, he lost his house and he is separated from his children.

When Monica visited home from rehab on an overnight stay I told her, "Take some steps so I can see where you are." She took four or five steps on her own without me holding her, bracing her up, or supporting her. After that, I had her in training camp to support her healing at home.

My wife is strong and her faith is solid.

Monica and I do what we have to do and together we are still standing.

Discharged and Life was Different

March 2013

On March 1, 2013, I was discharged from Metro Rehabilitation Facility where I received what I thought was pretty good care. It was finally time to sleep in my own bed. I wasn't sure whether or not I could maneuver in and out without assistance, but I was hopeful. I knew that my priority would be to focus on a plan to build my strength, stamina and endurance.

I thought it should be first on my agenda to schedule outpatient physical therapy at South Pointe. This was significant to continue my recovery. I had undergone therapy at South Pointe before, so I was familiar with their therapists and I was elated to work with them again.

I felt confident that I would be able to make progress with the therapeutic goals and objectives established. The therapist and I always seemed to connect. I think the fact that our personalities jived well was a plus. This time around, therapy was a bit more challenging. I was ambulating with a walker and not a quad cane and that made things more physically difficult with my legs. The steadiness on my feet just wasn't present.

I am not sure how, but I persisted and got through a number of sessions with her. My therapist suggested a walker early on to help me maintain what is called, ". . . normal walking stride." Of course I didn't recall her suggestion, but if in fact she did suggest the walker, I'm sure

I couldn't see the benefit at the time. It was hard enough to walk with a quad cane let alone a walker. I wasn't ready!

After being discharged from the rehab facility, a nurse come to check on me at my home when I was taking the Rebif injections. On one of her visits she noticed that my right foot was dragging. "You don't seem to be steady on your feet. Maybe you could use a walker." My mom went to a local pharmacy and purchased my first shiny red walker.

The first time I used my walker I met my friend at our favorite submarine sandwich restaurant. At the time I was still driving so when I got out of the car I felt strange walking with the walker. What I felt may be the same discomfort people feel when someone is kind and holds the door for them! I would trade in my strange and uncomfortable feelings from back then for where I am now. These are the days I look back and appreciate my journey.

***

Starting out I would be in therapy twice a week although outpatient was not as intensive as inpatient rehab. I recognized that therapy was helpful to my overall strength. My daily schedule would not be nearly as busy as I thought, so I worked from home. I was thankful that I had a computer to complete my normal tasks. I continued to assist my coworkers by generating ideas for weekly activities and designing the monthly calendar with graphics and themes. I enjoyed being creative in that way.

My direct supervisor had always been understanding from day one. She is a woman of faith and believed in prayer. How awesome was that to have that quality in a supervisor? This strong lady had three family members living with Multiple Sclerosis! While working at Highland Hills I was blessed to have met them all. I looked at all of them as living testimonies of how God is a keeper!

Even though my job asked me to come back to work out of the office, I knew that I wasn't ready. To tell the truth, I was a bit uncomfortable using a walker and no longer wanted the weight of multiple responsibilities. With the walker my pace was a lot slower. I did not think using a walker would have been as easy to use in an office setting.

I recognized that safety was my first priority, and even though I maintained my driver's license, I wasn't comfortable behind the wheel of a car. I definitely did not want my inability to drive to be part of my new normal. Being mindful of the safety of others was important to me so I did not drive.

When I was out with my husband it was nice to be chauffeured by him. I was used to getting out and going where I wanted to go, when I wanted to go and doing other things. I was used to going to the grocery store and even cooking dinner. Thankfully Tony is a great cook and he stepped in where I fell short.

September 2013

I was extremely disappointed and found it hard to believe that five months after my discharge date I found myself readmitted to Metro Rehabilitation on August 28, 2013. Unfortunately, I was a repeat offender in a sarcastic way!

The seasons were starting to change and we were in the month of September. This time around my exacerbation included visual changes. Things looked hazy and gloomy. I was not able to see clearly. I could see faces but distinguishing them challenging. Staff names were familiar, but I could not read name tags. The building was familiar, but without normal vision, I felt like I was in foreign territory. I could not see, or read the calendar in my room. I relied heavily on staff to help me.

The daily routines were pretty much the same. I believe this factor helped considerably as I began rehab again. When I entered the therapy room, I was introduced to a new physical therapist, but my former therapist was there too. For the first 15 minutes we focused on increasing my endurance and stamina with an assigned walker. For the next 15 minutes I rode the stationary bike. This therapeutic bike helped my feet propel the petals and I really did need the assistance.

I had more strength in my upper extremities. I enjoyed occupational therapy more than physical therapy. Usage of the therapeutic clay reminded me of Play-Doh when I was a child and I was able to practice my handwriting. I liked the bean bag toss for the game of Tic-Tac-Toe. Although last in my description of activities, memory game cards ranked high on my list of favorites!

Each day my progress improved with an increase in the number of steps I was able to take during physical therapy. I was examined by a podiatrist who recommended an ankle-foot orthosis, or AFO, which effectively cradles the ankle joint and forces the foot into a heel-to-toe motion. It is not uncommon that many people with MS wear AFOs on one or two feet.

I must admit during my second rehab stay I played the role of patient and social worker! After my therapy sessions and sometimes even in between I made phone calls and left messages when necessary!

I was under the care of a neurologist who was not on staff at Metro and as a result I had to make a lot of telephone calls. Due to my second relapse that particular year, it was obvious my current medication was not working as well as it should. I was being referred to my doctor's colleague at Cleveland Clinic Mellen Center for MS. I wasn't sure of a discharge date, but securing an appointment was my first priority.

I was able to make an appointment that coincided with my October discharge date. I praised God for His intervention and sovereignty! The new neurologist suggested that I try Tysabri, a newer MS medication on the market. He thought it might work better. Due to the documented side effects of this weekly infusion I hoped I wouldn't be a good candidate.

Tony and I met with the new neurologist. There were blood tests taken to confirm yay or nay on the medication. Thank you Jesus! It was a no-go and this expert recommended Tecfidera, an oral pill taken twice a day. This would be my second attempt at an oral medication, but I held on to my belief that God is able!

The physical therapist was the first to schedule a home visit. She conducted the initial assessment and determined my needs for occupational therapy. I accomplished the simple exercises with ease that tested the strength of my upper body. However, my ability to use my lower extremities was challenged.

I walked from one end to the other in the hallway of my building using a walker. The hallways are rather long so it was important that I was able to pace myself while moving and taking breaks when necessary. When the occupational therapist visited, I enjoyed her therapy much more. We did a balloon toss that challenged my standing balance skills. We used therapy putty to exercise my fine motor skills, it reminded me of the clay I played with as a child. The reality is that therapists can give examples of what to do but when they are gone, how committed are you to do the things necessary?!

After my case was closed I decided to call the occupational therapist to come out for a recap. This was in the year of 2015. I thought I was doing well physically and strength-wise and I had been on the new medication for two years. My therapist commented, "You are doing well. What are you doing exactly?"

I had to admit, "I am not utilizing the strategies learned when we initially met, but I am on a new MS therapy that seems to be working well!"

Part III – Thank You Lord

Strength of Testimony

I consider myself to be a *doer* and not just a *hearer* of the word. Encouraged by the book of Revelations chapter 12:11, I thought it would be easy to encourage others to share their personal testimonies. I began sharing with a few sisters who were part of my prayer circle, the idea of hosting a women's fellowship.

I suggested that meetings could be hosted at my home on the third Saturday of each month at Noon. Bringing refreshments was optional, but most times I was able to supply light refreshments. Tony brought everything to the community room which made it easier for me.

Some ladies I asked willingly agreed to share their testimony, but others were not so agreeable. Refusing to be discouraged, I decided that I would be the first to share. I didn't want to be long-winded so I used the memo section of my phone to keep focus on what I wanted to say.

I was a little nervous, but bright smiles and from the ladies made me feel comfortable. As I begin to share, I couldn't help but focus on the faithfulness of my husband who was attending to my every need. "My husband worked a full-time job at a local car wash close to our home. He was extremely tired at the end of his workday but he maintained all of the household chores." I shared with the women that I knew in my heart that he readily relied each day on the Lord's strength! "Balancing work and visits to see me while I was in rehab was no easy feat. I was confident that he always did his best!"

I talked about my initial diagnosis of MS in 2001 and gave details that unfolded 12 years later. "Believe it or not," I told them, "I was actually admitted and discharged twice in 2013. I had never been hospitalized for an entire month at a time, but honestly it was a lot for us to handle mentally and emotionally."

I shared with the women, "I couldn't believe that rehab was my home away from home." I imagine the late night telephone calls weren't easy for Tony either, but I needed to hear his voice for the soothing and calming effects. "Love is definitely an action word. It is patient. Love is kind. Love never fails and it is so amazing."

For the second fellowship one of my prayer partners agreed to share her testimony. She and her mom were both breast cancer survivors. What an abundance of God's grace in this family. This sister shared that her granddaughter recognized and felt her lump, which propelled her to visit her doctor. It was such an encouraging testimony and reminded me that God is no respecter of persons. What He does for one He is able to do for another!

As the word began to spread about the meetings, other ladies began to participate and share their individual stories. I believe that for women it is important to recognize that we are not alone in the trials and tribulations that come in life. By sharing, we all take a stance. Fighting against all odds we must continue to stand on the Word of

God, We must believe that it is true and our faith will strengthen as a result.

We can't forget that as we stand on our faith, we stand on the shoulders of mothers and grandmothers, and aunts and teachers, mentors and pastors who continue to lead the way.

I Still Believe God

Some people come to Christ without family influence, but both my grandmother and mother were Women of Faith. I accepted Jesus Christ as my personal Lord and Savior early in life. My mother used to send me to Sunday School and Vacation Bible School on a church bus. The Bible says in Proverbs 22:6, "Train up a child in the way that they should go and when they are old they will not depart" I believe this scripture was their motto for the children in my family.

My grandmother's father was a minister. My entire family was raised in the church because of his Godly influence! Jesus made the ultimate sacrifice by dying on the cross. Living for Him because of His sacrifice is a challenge we all must embrace!

I was learning about God and the Bible at an early age with my mom. Being a twelve year old girl, I saw other young girls around my age shouting and dancing in the spirit. I wondered why they were experiencing something I had not experienced.

I knew that I wanted God to lead me. I knew even from some of the things I learned from my Grandmother that I wanted to know God. Even our pastor at the time, Pastor Harris, made the Word of God easy for any age to understand. One Sunday after he gave the call of salvation to accept Christ, I answered the call and said yes to His will for my life.

Through one of the Vacation Bible School lessons I learned that my name means "Advisor." When I got older, I recognized that even the career path I had chosen as a social worker was in the meaning of who God had made me with the name He called me.

It was fifteen years from the time I accepted Christ to the time I was given my MS diagnosis. Throughout those years I had been standing on scriptures and Proverbs 3:5-6 is one of my favorites. I would tell my twelve year old self , "Know that your relationship with God takes time, commitment, diligence and a desire to seek Him daily. Relax and enjoy the journey with God." The revelation I have at 45, is that my faith has been an ongoing process.

I have had different experiences in my life that have taught me who God is. This is about my relationship with God and my faith. Romans 10:17 says, "So then faith cometh by hearing, and hearing by the word of God." Pray and be open to God using you as you grow and experience Him. This will help you reach a different level of maturity.

Trusting God early gave me the tenacity to stand against some of life's greatest challenges as I matured in age! Many of my earliest experiences came with both challenge and excitement. Even though the total manifestation of my healing has not happened yet, I still believe God. I know that He is able to do exceedingly and abundantly above all that I can ask or think. I am patiently waiting and I am still standing on my faith.

I may bend but I definitely won't break. I haven't been able to walk with my quad cane because my balance is a little shaky, but I am still standing. Sometimes Aunt Arlene encourages me by saying, "Run Forrest." It does encourage me; I believe in my heart that my healing is a process. I am thanking and praising God in advance for it.

As I trust God each day, I feel my breakthrough. My body naturally responds to stress by demonstrating a fight or flight response. I would have to say that I consider myself a fighter. I am confident about this distinction because I use prayer and praise as my weapons! I know this battle is not mine, but it is my opportunity to give God all glory, honor and praise. He deserves it!

A lot of people in my inner circle have expressed that they believe I experienced denial with my MS diagnosis. I don't think Aunt Arlene was the first person to say that to me. I used to respond, "How can you be in denial of something that you don't really understand?" I thank God because I have better comprehension of how MS effects my body. I know He has been with me through the process.

I am thankful because I feel like God can use me to help others believe there is nothing too hard for Him. I want people to keep their faith, keep praying, fasting and trusting – God is not a man that He should lie. God honors His Word. If I am the chosen vessel for Him to spread this message, I am grateful. If I had never been diagnosed with MS, I would never be able to say that with confidence and assurance.

When my total manifestation of healing comes to the surface, I will be amazed. We can see God working while we go through the process, but we must think clearly and say to ourselves, "God had entrusted me with this opportunity and experience. I am His vessel." We can't give up or lose heart, God is in control even when we can't see Him at work.

Holding on to Hope

As 2019 was coming to an end, my dear friend Elana Siggers, invited me to her church's first Women's Conference. She was part of the conference committee. Elana and I grew up at Mt. Olive Missionary Baptist Church so seeing her work cooperatively and diligently with other women was awesome. The theme of the conference was, "Dealing With Matters of the Heart" taken from Psalms 51:10. It had been a long time since I had attended a conference, so I was elated.

Friday evening was relaxed with a meet and greet. It truly felt like a family reunion. Saturday the conference had three speakers. Each of them presented in their own unique way. I thoroughly enjoyed their presentations along with participant discussion. Many shared their personal testimonies and I feel that we need more opportunities like this for people to share. Again, this is how we overcome!

During this conference I won a prize and wanted Elana's mom, whom I call "Auntie Sharon," to pick out my prize. She insisted, "You can do it on your own." I picked out a cushioned stress ball, which reminded me of something I used in physical therapy. I found this ball to be extra special because is spelled out the word "hope!" Yes, I'm definitely holding onto positive expectations and every time I squeeze the ball it will be a reminder. This is what my hope stands for everyday! I expect God to do exceedingly abundantly above all that I can ask or think.

Don't lose hope!

When I was in therapy, I reflected on the song written by Reverend Clay Evans entitled, "I've Got a Testimony." The lyrics remind me of my own testimony and blessings. I marveled about the great memories I had from childhood that required agility, balance and coordination.

When I think about the things I could do prior to my MS diagnosis, I am amazed. I was a gymnast; walking on a balance beam and then flipping off it. I jumped double-dutch. I played kickball and tag. I learned how to do cartwheels by watching others do them.

The older girls in the neighborhood did cheers like they were already on a cheering squad and I learned them as well. L-O-V-E was my first cheer. "Monica is my name; love is my game..." When I was in the Warrensville school district, I was on the sixth-grade gymnastic team. I became a junior varsity and varsity cheerleader. I was captain of the Varsity squad my senior year. I was in school talent shows modeling with heels on my feet. I even tried out for the track team, but I didn't make it. It did not discourage me; I was once told "nothing beats a failure but a try!" Those were fond memories of some of my early days.

Instead of complaining about the things I can no longer do, I recognize that God has given me a myriad of memories. The best thing about memories is the fact that they last a lifetime. I rejoice and celebrate with this thought in mind, "Thank you Jesus for what you've already done in my life and for what you continue to do!"

Bless the Lord, O my soul: and all that is within me, bless his holy name. Bless the Lord, O my soul, and forget not all his benefits: Who forgiveth all thine iniquities;
who healeth all thy diseases . . .
Psalm 103:1-4 (KJV)

". . .thank you Jesus for what you've already done in my life and for what you continue to do!"

−Monica D. Rushton

MS is a disease that effects my ability to stand in the physical. I once walked with a quad cane and I was once able to stand. Now I am walking with a walker, and I am still standing. I use a wheelchair in public because it is easier for me to get around. I can get out of the chair and I can stand. It is a bit emotional for me to think of "Still Standing" as a declaration, yet I have been using it for a long time.

A Faith Experience

God taught me how to walk in faith during a concert of prayer at my church one year. This lesson in faith has sustained me over the years. That day the altar was open for prayer for 24 hours a day. I was able to go early one morning and kneel before the altar. While I was kneeling in prayer the Holy Spirit spoke to me and said, "Man is not your source."

During the season of prayer, our pastor asked for us to give a seed offering in faith. I was not working at the time and my cousin was giving me $100 monthly. Since I did not have much income that seed helped me pay my car note. I heard the Holy Spirit tell me to sow a faith seed of $100. I don't know how that amount of money was ever recouped, but I know that my car note was paid that month. God revealed Philippians 4:19 in a way that I never knew before.

I try to hold on to that memory even as financial challenges come and go. My husband and I trust Him as we tithe and give where He leads us to give.

I want you to know friends, that you can stand in the strength and the power of Jesus. His strength is made perfect in weakness. Although MS makes people feel weak, healing has been a process. From a spiritual perspective I am standing on the true Word of God. I have given you scriptures throughout the book that I have been standing on. I want you to read them in different versions to help you study God's Word. Here are a few more:

- Psalm 103
- Revelations 12:11
- 1 Peter 5:10
- 3 John 2
- Isaiah 54:17
- Matthew 9:22
- Romans 8:37

Recently I shared with someone that I often feel needy. I cannot attribute looking up the definition to any other reason than being led by the Holy Spirit. The description I found says: "(of a person) lacking the necessities of life; very poor."

Today I recognize that I was using the word incorrectly. I actually use that word because I'm unable to do things for my myself that I used to do independently. The reality is that everybody needs help sometimes. I shared that when I was in rehab I painted a butterfly in art therapy. I learned later that an MRI of the brain is shaped like a butterfly.

God has given me this season with Multiple Sclerosis to pray more, accept the things I cannot change and to trust Him at His Word. I can declare that He is not a man that He should lie. I felt that if I went off to college and got a decent-paying job I'd be able to take care of myself as a self-sufficient independent African American woman! What I have learned is that God is in control.

In Haggai 2:9 the Bible says, "The glory of this latter house shall be greater than of the former, saith the Lord of hosts: and in this place will I give peace, saith the Lord of hosts." I think of this scripture often. Before my mother passed away, one Christmas she gave me a t-shirt with the words "Never give up" across the front. When I saw those words, I broke down in tears which turned into laughter; it felt good to release my feelings in that moment.

That t-shirt given confirmed that my mother was praying for me and believed God with me. She wanted me to know God is able.

My husband gave me a bracelet that is inscribed with the words "Never give up" on one side and "Never quit" on the other. I wear this bracelet as a reminder to stay my course. I cherish all of these reminders to keep standing on my faith. I stand amazed.

It is almost like I can still hear my mother saying, "Never give up daughter." Now, I want to declare this statement to all of you: Never Give Up!

For our light affliction, which is but for a moment, worketh for us a far more exceeding and eternal weight of glory;
II Corinthians 4:17 (KJV)

Dear Sisters and Brothers,

Thank you for taking the time to read my story. I appreciate you!

I want to encourage, motivate, and empower you to continue to press forward while on the life journey designed specifically for you! Yes, there will be challenges that seem hard, but try to remember the race is not given to those who are wanting to make it to the finish line quickly. The victory awaits those who will endure the process with hope, patience and faith.

Trust the process. God has ordained specifications for your story with you in mind. If you have Multiple Sclerosis like me, or some other physical, emotional or spiritual challenge, don't give up! With all of your might, strength, and hope; trust and believe!

There is nothing too hard for God and His power!

Peace and blessings always,

Monica

God is not man, that he should lie, or a son of man, that he should change his mind. Has he said, and will he not do it?
Or has he spoken, and will he not fulfill it?
Numbers 23:19

"I stand amazed!"

-Monica D. Rushton

About the Author

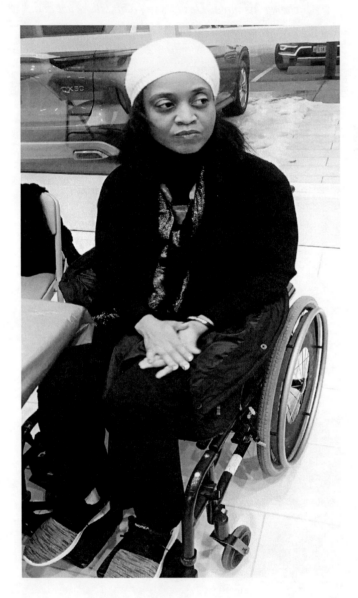

Monica Denay Rushton is a former licensed social worker. Her diverse work experience is in management, assessment and development. Having worked in a variety of settings including nonprofit community-based centers, elementary schools and hospitals, she has developed an increased sense of empathy for others! Her work opportunities have broadened her perspective, giving her multicultural experiences as she's worked with individuals and families.

Monica's greatest desire is to be an instrument used by God. She wants to share hope and courage that will inspire others to believe that no matter what they are going through, all things are possible with mustard seed faith.

Acknowledgments

Heavenly Father: You are first. Tony and I stand on Proverbs 3:5-6. You are so amazing. You deserve all of my praise, all of my honor, all of my thanksgiving and gratitude. All of what I have is due to You. Without You I am nothing.

To my Honey Bun Tony: Thank you is not enough for your encouragement, your personal determination and your drive to see this project come to life. You told my mother, "You don't have to worry, I will take care of her," and you have kept your promise. I love you.

To the Rushton Family: Thank you for your support on this journey.

Marlon and Monique: I can't imagine my life without you. You bring so much unexplainable joy to me. I am proud to call you my little brother and sister. We share a bond that can never be broken! When I think of you Patti Labelle's song, "You are my Friend" plays in my heart. I love you always and forever

To my Aunts: you are all my favorite. Thank you for your prayers along my journey and for your encouragement all of my life.

Aunt Arlene: You have been my secretary for a long time and I appreciate the help you provided while I was writing *Still Standing*.

Cousin David: Thank you is not enough for all you have done, for all you have given, and for all of the mountains you have helped me climb!

To my Thornton Condominium Neighbors: Carolyn Oates, Michelle Oppenheimer and Janice Williams, thank you for your encouragement, your love and your support.

My Prayer Warriors and Unpluckable Faith Community: It is often said that good friends are hard to find. You are all blessings from God. I am extremely blessed to have some awesome women in my life: Amber Culbreath, Gina Johnston, Senequa Poteat, Sherelle Clark, Connie Strong, Debra Hairston, True Motley, Bessie Williams, Ann Todd, Evelyn Minah, Jessica Hall, Sharon Thompson, Laverne Walls, Pastor Lori of the prayer ministry team known as H O P, Elana Siggers, Ebony Broussard, Francis Lipscomb and Kendra Petite. The prayers of a the righteous availeth much.

To my Family (Too many others to name): My love is forever yours. The Bible says, "We love because He first loved us." I am grateful to be the first family author.

Coach P. and InSCRIBEd Inspiration: Without you there would be no *Still Standing*. This has been an amazing experience. I am truly blessed that we were connected "for such a time as this!"

The Bible says that children are a gift from God. I absolutely agree! I am blessed to be an Aunt to Monique's daughters. Where do I begin to express the joy that these three little girls have brought into my life? You complete my cupcake box; vanilla, chocolate and strawberry – Mmm Good! Love you, Auntie Monica.

Jiani: You have been my little lady from the time you arrived. You always demonstrate helpfulness in your childlike innocence. When you were asked, "How does it feel to know that Auntie Monica needs your help sometimes?" It warmed my heart to know that you think it's ok.

Janii: You once said, " I feel sad because I want Auntie Monica to be normal like us!" Sweet baby I feel sad sometimes too. I try to stay strong and trust God through this process to turn circumstances around — God has already demonstrated His power and virtue to heal, set free, and deliver me. It's just a matter of time before receiving my miraculous breakthrough!

Jayci Denay: You have a special place in my heart as my namesake! Born at 7lbs 11oz, you will always be my 7/11 baby.

I LOVE MY FAMILY

I wanted to share a photos of a few special people in my life who have helped me stand:

1.)   Amber, Ebony and I after we won first place in a college talent show (circa 1994).
2.)   My groom in Vegas (July 27, 2012)
3.)   My beloved Grandma and I on her birthday (circa 2003)
4.)   My mother and I celebrating my birthday

Many are the afflictions of the righteous:
but the Lord delivereth him out of them all.
Psalm 34:19 - KJV

"Stick to your plan."

-Monica D. Rushton

STILL Standing

MAKING *Progress* THROUGH THE *Process*